NATIVE AMERICAN NATIONS

THE NAVAJO

BY BETTY MARCKS

CONSULTANT: TIM TOPPER, CHEYENNE RIVER SIOUX

BLASTOFF! DISCOVERY

BELLWETHER MEDIA • MINNEAPOLIS, MN

Author's Statement of Positionality:
I am a white woman of European descent. As such, I can claim no direct lived experience of being a Native American. In writing this book, however, I have tried to be an ally by relying on sources by Native American writers and authors whenever possible and have worked to let their voices guide its content.

This edition first published in 2024 by Bellwether Media, Inc.

Library of Congress Cataloging-in-Publication Data

Names: Marcks, Betty, author.
Title: The Navajo / by Betty Marcks.
Description: Minneapolis, MN : Bellwether Media, Inc., 2024. | Series: Blastoff! Discovery : Native American nations | Includes bibliographical references and index. | Audience: Ages 7-13 | Audience: Grades 4-6 | Summary: "Engaging images accompany information about the Navajo. The combination of high-interest subject matter and narrative text is intended for students in grades 3 through 8" – Provided by publisher.
Identifiers: LCCN 2023023100 (print) | LCCN 2023023101 (ebook) | ISBN 9798886874433 (library binding) | ISBN 9798886876314 (ebook)
Subjects: CYAC: Navajo Indians
Classification: LCC E99.N3 M384 2024 (print) | LCC E99.N3 (ebook) | DDC 979.1004/9726–dc23/eng/20230607
LC record available at https://lccn.loc.gov/2023023100
LC ebook record available at https://lccn.loc.gov/2023023101

Editor: Elizabeth Neuenfeldt   Series Designer: Andrea Schneider
Book Designer: Laura Sowers

Printed in the United States of America, North Mankato, MN.

TABLE OF

CONTENTS

THE GLITTERING WORLD

The Navajo are a nation of Native American peoples. They call themselves *Diné*. It means "The People." The **origin** story of the Navajo states the Diné were created from corn in *Dinétah*. Dinétah is the Navajo's homeland.

Dinétah lies within the four **Sacred** Mountains. It is part of the Fifth World known as "The Glittering World." Navajo stories say the First Man went through Four Worlds before finding the Fifth World. Dinétah spans the **Four Corners** region of today's Southwestern United States. It includes parts of Utah, Colorado, New Mexico, and Arizona.

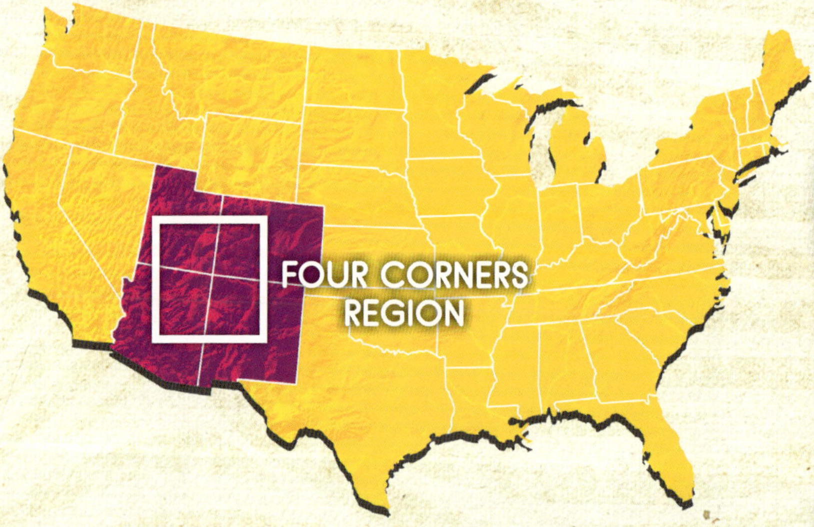

THE NAVAJO NATION

The Navajo Nation has the largest population and land of any Native American nation in the U.S.

TRADITIONAL NAVAJO LIFE

The Navajo origin story states that the god Changing Woman, Asdzą́ą́ Nádleehé, created the original four Navajo **clans**. Clans give each person their identity. The clan system is **matrilineal**. Each person belongs to four clans. Their first clan is through their mother. The other three are through their father and grandparents.

INSIDE A HOGAN

Families often lived near the woman's family. They built hogans. Some people live in hogans today. These homes may be dome-shaped. They are often made of logs or stones covered with mud or dirt. The door faces the rising sun in the east. Some do not have windows or rooms. Hogans are also used for **ceremonies**.

Dinétah is in a mostly dry climate. It is made up of deserts, canyons, and cool mountains. This varied landscape provided food and resources to the Navajo's **ancestors**. The Navajo were hunters and gatherers before the 1600s. They hunted large animals such as elk and bighorn sheep. They collected fruits and plants.

The Navajo learned how to farm from neighboring **Pueblo** peoples. They grew corn, squash, fruit, and many other crops. The Spanish introduced sheep and herding in the 1500s. The Navajo's ancestors became expert sheep herders. They relied on the animals' meat, milk, and wool.

CANYON DE CHELLY

The Canyon de Chelly is important Navajo farming land. The Navajo's ancestors grew corn, pumpkins, beans, peaches, and other crops in the canyon. Navajo farmers mostly grow peaches in the area today.

NAVAJO RESOURCES

SHEEP

MEAT

MILK

WOOL BLANKETS, CLOTHING, AND RUGS

The Navajo's ancestors became skilled weavers. The god Spider Man showed the people how to make the loom. The god Spider Woman taught them how to weave. Weaving wool became a sacred practice. **Geometric** designs stand for important parts of Navajo life and religion.

Corn also plays an important role in Navajo **culture**. It is used in ceremonies and **traditions**. Corn cakes are cooked for coming-of-age ceremonies for girls. Corn pollen is often used in prayer.

WEAVING WOOL

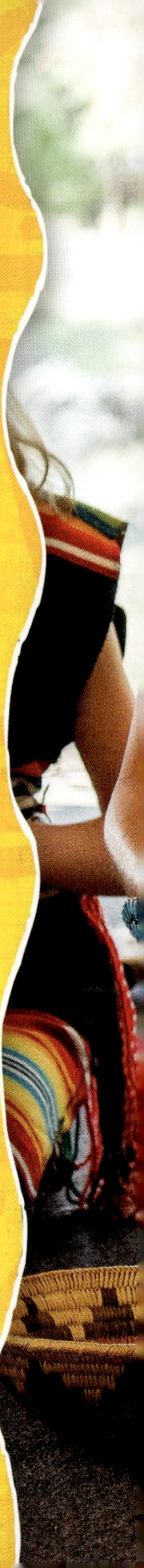

TRADITIONAL CORN GRINDING AT THE NAVAJO FESTIVAL OF ARTS AND CULTURE

JOSÉ ANTONIO VIZCARRA, A MEXICAN SOLDIER WHO FOUGHT AGAINST THE NAVAJO IN THE 1820s

Life in the Southwest changed when the Spanish arrived in the 1500s. They conquered many of the peoples. But they did not defeat the Navajo. Mexico claimed Navajo land in 1821. They **enslaved** Navajo women and children. But the Navajo continued to fight back.

The U.S. government claimed control of Navajo land in 1848. The Navajo tried to make peace with the U.S. But **settlers** moved onto their land. The Navajo resisted the U.S. government's attempts to control them. The Navajo also defended themselves against neighboring Native American nations.

NAVAJO ROCK ART SHOWING CONFLICT WITH THE UTE

In 1863, the U.S. government ordered Christopher "Kit" Carson to destroy the Navajo way of life. Carson and his troops destroyed Navajo homes. They also destroyed important resources such as sheep. Some Navajo escaped. Others were forced to march hundreds of miles to a camp called Bosque Redondo. The march became known as the Long Walk.

FAMOUS NAVAJO

CHIEF MANUELITO

BIRTHDAY 1818

DEATH 1893

FAMOUS FOR

Navajo chief who fought against the U.S. government's forced removal of Navajo people from their homeland and signed the Treaty of 1868 giving the Navajo some of their land back

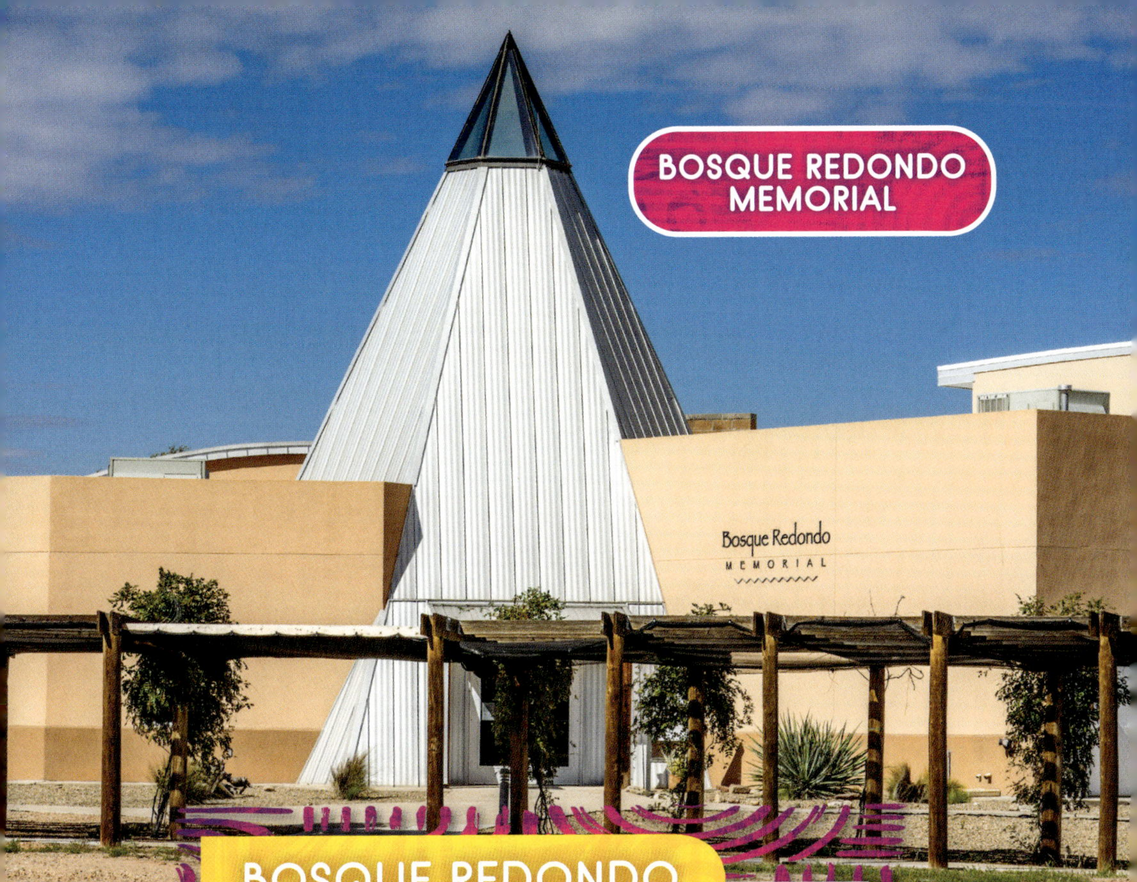

BOSQUE REDONDO

The Navajo call the Bosque Redondo camp *Hwéeldi*. It means "the place of great sorrow."

Chief Barboncito and Chief Manuelito signed a **treaty** giving their people back a small piece of their land in 1868. More of their land was returned to them over time. The current limits to the Navajo Nation **reservation** were declared in 1934.

LIFE TODAY

Today, the Navajo Nation covers about 27,000 square miles (69,930 square kilometers). It includes parts of Utah, Arizona, and New Mexico.

The Navajo Nation has around 400,000 members. Around 170,000 members live on the Nation's land. Other members live in different places around the world. Some people carry on the traditions of farming and ranching on the reservation. People own businesses both on and off Navajo land. Members are also teachers, lawyers, mechanics, and much more.

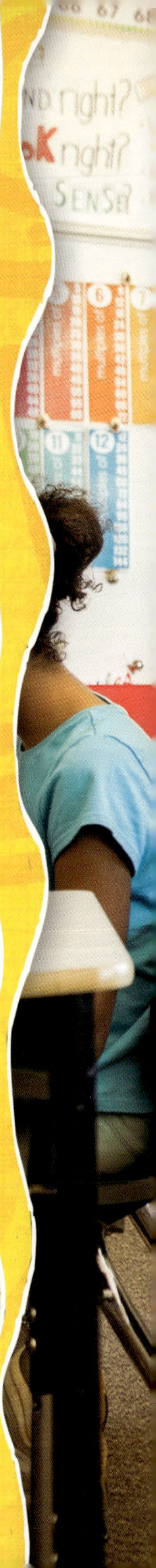

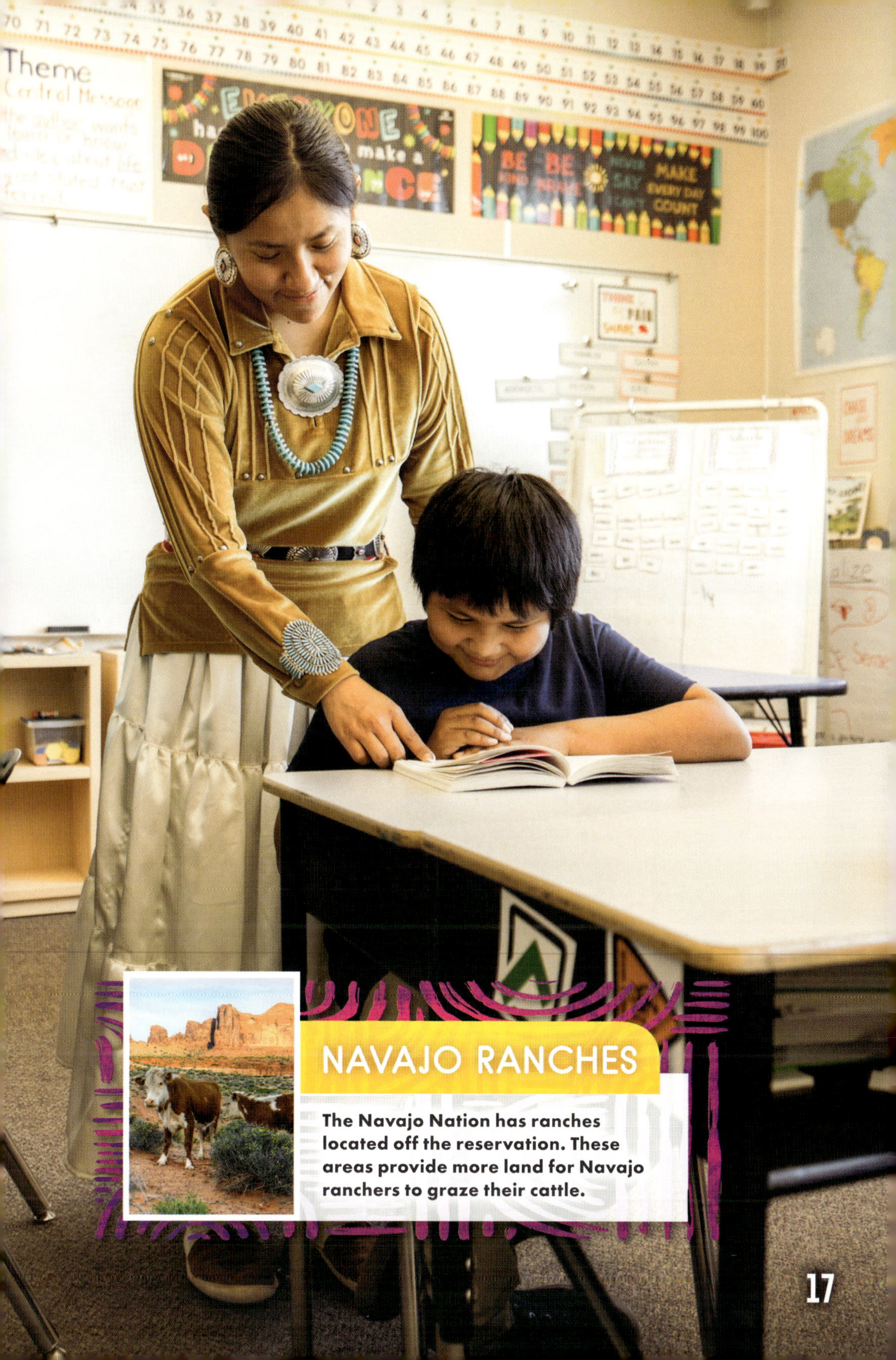

NAVAJO RANCHES

The Navajo Nation has ranches located off the reservation. These areas provide more land for Navajo ranchers to graze their cattle.

The Navajo Nation has a three-branch government. It works for the people. The government is led by a President and Vice President. The Navajo Nation **Council** is made up of 24 members who represent the people. They vote on laws. The Nation's courts include the Supreme Court and district courts. They also have a Peacekeeping Program. It resolves issues between people through traditional Diné teachings.

GOVERNMENT OF THE NAVAJO NATION

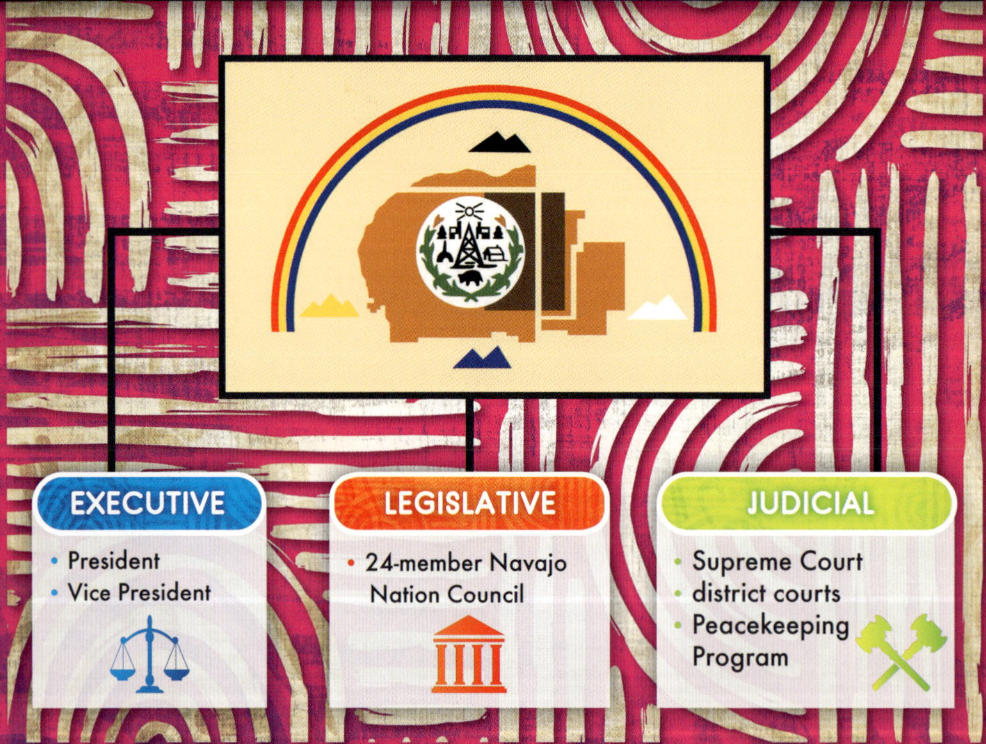

NAVAJO NATION PRESIDENT, BUU VAN NYGREN

The government works to keep the Navajo Nation strong as it grows. It provides health care, education, and other services to members of the Navajo Nation.

CONTINUING TRADITIONS

NECKLACE WITH NAJA DESIGN

Many Navajo artists practice the traditions of their ancestors. Some artists use silver and turquoise to create jewelry. A common style of necklace includes a *Naja*, or "curved," design. Basket weaving uses a coil method. Traditional colors include white, black, and red. But artists today may use more colors.

Blanket and rug weavers include traditional geometric designs. Natural colors such as indigo and brown hues are common. Other artists choose to introduce new ideas. They use untraditional dyes including yellow, purple, and turquoise. Ancestral Navajo raised churro sheep. Some modern weavers choose to raise these sheep for their wool.

NAVAJO WEAVING SYMBOLS

Navajo weavers often weave designs into blankets and rugs. Designs can have special meanings.

CROSS
SPIDER WOMAN, PROTECTOR OF THE NAVAJO

DIAMOND
DINÉTAH, NAVAJO HOMELAND

ZIGZAGS
LIGHTNING AND POWER

The U.S. government carried out a program to cut the numbers of Navajo livestock. Nearly all churro sheep were gone after the program was completed. Today, a program called the Navajo Sheep Project works to increase the number of churro sheep. It teaches people about the cultural importance of churro sheep. It also improves the lives of ranchers and weavers.

The Navajo Nation hosts events each year to celebrate culture and traditions. People practice traditional song and dance at the annual Central Navajo Fair. A rodeo showcases centuries of horsemanship skills. The Navajo Nation Fair displays artists' arts and crafts.

CHURRO SHEEP

TRADITIONAL WEAVING DEMONSTRATION, NAVAJO NATION FAIR

NAVAJO CODE TALKERS

More than 400 Navajo served as Code Talkers during World War II. The Navajo Code Talkers created a code in the Navajo language. They used the code to send secret military messages. The Japanese military could not understand the code.

FIGHT TODAY, BRIGHT TOMORROW

DRIED UP LAKE DUE TO DROUGHT, NAVAJO NATION

The Navajo and other Native American nations of the Southwest have lived well in the dry climate for thousands of years. But the region has been in a **drought** since the early 1990s. The Navajo Nation has struggled to access clean water.

Around one-third of people living on the Navajo reservation do not have access to clean water. Thousands of people are forced to get water from stations miles from their homes. Farmers and ranchers do not have enough water for their crops and livestock.

The Navajo Nation has been fighting for water rights for decades. But the U.S. government is not considering many of the Navajo Nation's needs. Navajo leaders went to the U.S. Supreme Court to argue their rights to safe water in 2023.

CEREMONY RECOGNIZING WATER RIGHTS TO THE NAVAJO NATION IN UTAH IN 2022

The Nation has also created plans to fight the issues related to the drought. Some of the plans include water supply projects. The Western Navajo Pipeline project would use water from Lake Powell in northern Arizona. The Navajo Nation has experienced greatness and hardship. The Nation is growing, and their traditions will live on!

TIMELINE

1500s

The Navajo have their first contact with the Spanish

1821

Mexico claims Navajo land

1846

The U.S. declares war on Mexico and the Navajo meet members of the U.S. military for the first time

1863 TO 1866

Thousands of Navajo peoples are forced to walk hundreds of miles to the Bosque Redondo in what becomes known as the Long Walk

1868

Chief Barboncito and Chief Manuelito sign the Navajo Treaty of 1868, allowing the people to return to a small area of their original land

1934

The current land area of the Navajo Nation is declared

1968

The Navajo Tribal Council names the reservation the Navajo Nation, and Diné College opens, the first Native American-operated Tribal college in the U.S.

1923

The Navajo tribal government is created

2023

Navajo leaders go to the U.S. Supreme Court to argue for their rights to use the Colorado River to access clean water

1942 TO 1945

The Navajo Code Talkers send secret U.S. military information by telephone and radio messages in the Navajo language during World War II

GLOSSARY

ancestors–relatives who lived long ago

ceremonies–sets of actions performed in a particular way, often as part of religious worship

clans–groups of people who share a common ancestor

council–a group of people who meet to run a government

culture–the beliefs, arts, and ways of life in a place or society

drought–an extended period of time with little to no rainfall

enslaved–considered someone property and forced them to work for no pay

Four Corners–the area in the Southwestern United States where Colorado, New Mexico, Arizona, and Utah come together

geometric–relating to straight or curved lines and shapes often used in designs

matrilineal–related to or based on following a family line through the mother

origin–beginning

Pueblo–relating to a group of peoples originating in the American Southwest, including the Hopi, the Zuni, and others

reservation–land set aside by the U.S. government for the forced removal of a Native American community from their original land

sacred–relating to religion

settlers–people who move to live in a new region

traditions–customs, ideas, and beliefs handed down from one generation to the next

treaty–an official agreement between two groups

TO LEARN MORE

AT THE LIBRARY

Bird, F.A. *Navajo.* Minneapolis, Minn.: Abdo Publishing, 2022.

Buckley, James, Jr. *Who Were the Navajo Code Talkers?* New York, N.Y.: Penguin Workshop, 2021.

Sonneborn, Liz. *The Hopi.* Minneapolis, Minn.: Bellwether Media, 2024.

ON THE WEB

FACTSURFER

Factsurfer.com gives you a safe, fun way to find more information.

1. Go to www.factsurfer.com.
2. Enter "the Navajo" into the search box and click 🔍.
3. Select your book cover to see a list of related content.

INDEX

The images in this book are reproduced through the courtesy of: grandriver/ Getty Images, front cover; Joseph Sohm, p. 3; Jane Rix, pp. 4-5; David P. Smith, p. 5; Ami Parikh, pp. 6-7; Hemis/ Alamy, p. 7; Nadia Yong, p. 8; Rinus Baak, p. 8 (Navajo rock art of corn); Danita Delimont/ Alamy, pp. 9 (peaches), 23; Tom Bean/ Alamy, pp. 9 (sheep), 22; margouillat photo, p. 9 (meat); Francesca Pianzola, p. 9 (milk); Gibon Art/ Alamy, pp. 9 (wool blankets, clothing, rugs), 21 (cross, zigzags); ClassicStock/ Alamy, p. 10; Juliana Swenson/ Alamy, pp. 10-11; unknown/ Wikipedia, pp. 12, 14, 18; Diane Johnson/ Alamy, p. 13; BHammond/ Alamy, p. 15; RichVintage, pp. 16-17; kojihirano, p. 17; AP/ AP Images, p. 19; Chuck Place/ Alamy, p. 20 (necklace); Scott Jones, p. 20; Rob Atkins/ Alamy, p. 21 (diamond); Everett Collection, p. 23 (Navajo Code Talkers); Spencer Platt/ Getty Images, pp. 24, 25; David McNew/ Getty Images, p. 25 (livestock water only); Associated Press/ AP Images, p. 26; davram, p. 27; U.S. Army Signal Corps/ Wikipedia, p. 28 (1863 to 1866); Alpha Historica/ Alamy, p. 29 (1942 to 1945); SLR Group/ Wikipedia, p. 29 (1968).